Winter

TAKE ONE

Claire Llewellyn

SIMON & SCHUSTER
YOUNG BOOKS

Notes for parents and teachers

This book has a theme that threads its way through the subject of the book. It does not aim to deal with the topic comprehensively; rather it aims to provoke thought and discussion. Each page heading makes a simple statement about the illustration which is then amplified and questioned by the text. Material in this book is particularly relevant to the following sections of the National Curriculum for England and Wales:

English: AT1 levels 1–2, AT2 levels 1–3
Geography: AT5 levels 1–3
Science: AT5 levels 1–3, AT9 levels 1–2, AT16 levels 1–3

In Scotland the proposals of the Scottish Education Department apply.

TAKE ONE has been researched and compiled by Simon & Schuster Young Books. We are very grateful for the support and guidance provided by our advisory panel of professional educationalists in the course of the production.

Advisory panel:
Colin Pidgeon, Headteacher
Wheatfields Junior School, St Albans
Deirdre Walker, Deputy headteacher
Wheatfields Junior School, St Albans
Judith Clarke, Headteacher
Grove Infants School, Harpenden

A catalogue record for this book is available from the British Library
ISBN 0 7500 1032 0

Commissioning editor: Daphne Butler
Design: M&M Design Partnership
Photographs: ZEFA except pages 7, 18, 26 and 27 Ecoscene; pages 19 and 23 (top) Heather Angel; page 11 Sally & Richard Greenhill; page 23 (bottom) Bruce Coleman/Wayne Lankinen
Line artwork: Raymond Turvey

First published in Great Britain in 1992 by Simon & Schuster Young Books

Simon & Schuster Young Books
Campus 400, Maylands Avenue
Hemel Hempstead, Herts HP2 7EZ

Printed and bound in Great Britain by BPCC Hazell Books, Paulton and Aylesbury

Contents

Winter is coming

How can you tell that winter is coming? It follows autumn but is quite different.

What changes does winter bring?

7

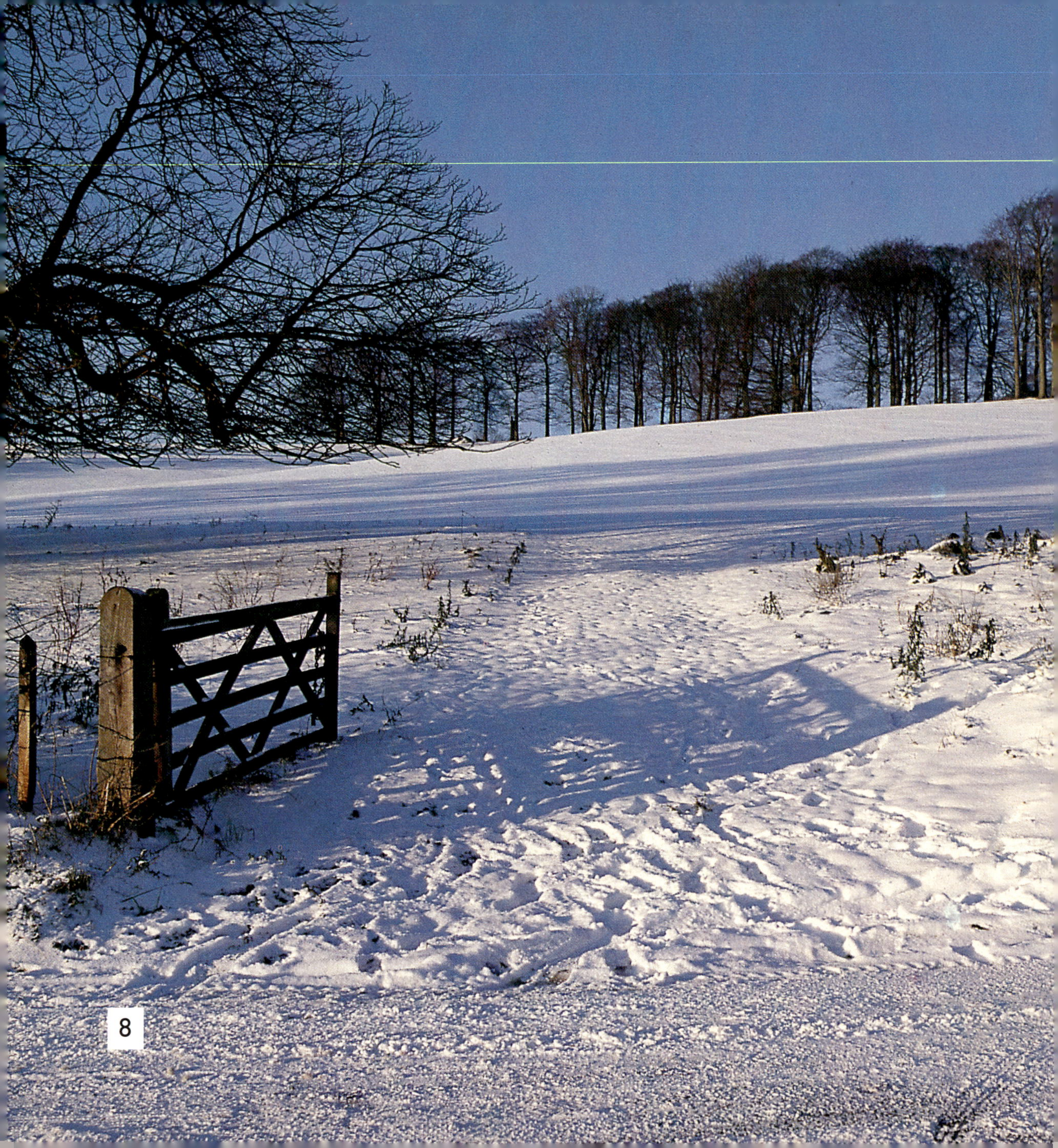

The days are getting shorter

In winter the mornings are dark. The sun is low in the sky, even in the middle of the day. Shadows are long.

On the other side of the world it's summer. Do you know why?

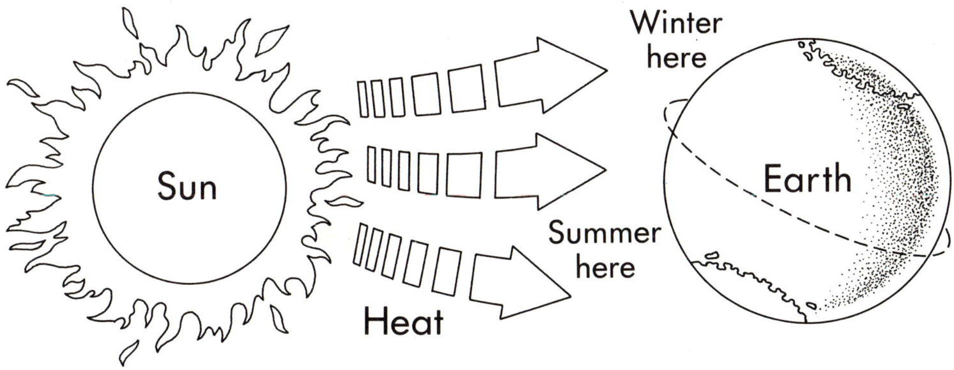

Which half of the Earth is tilted towards the sun?

Wintry weather

The days in winter are very cold.
The nights are frosty.
Cold winds bring rain and sleet.
Sometimes it even snows.

Where does it snow the most?
What problems can this cause?

Staying indoors

When it's cold outside, it's nice to settle down in a warm room with a book or a game.

Do you know how your home is heated? What else helps to keep your house snug in winter?

Keeping warm

Thick clothes keep the warm in and the cold out. Think about the clothes you wear in summer and winter. How are they different?

Eating a hot meal is another way to warm up on a cold winter's day. Our bodies burn up food, like a fire burns wood.

15

Keep moving!

Another way to keep warm in winter is to move – quickly!

Winter sports are fun, if there is plenty of snow. How many different sports can you think of?

Some people cannot move quickly. Who? How can they keep warm?

Animals need to keep warm

Winter weather is hard on animals. Some grow thicker coats to keep out the cold.

Birds have tiny bodies which are hard to keep warm. They fluff up their feathers. How does this help?

20

Food is scarce

Animals eat many different foods, such as seeds, fruit, worms, insects and fish. Many of these foods are hard to find in winter. Why?

Birds spend the whole day looking for food. How can you help them?

A winter rest

Snails and other mini beasts sleep through the cold weather in a safe, sheltered spot like a crack in a wall.

Some animals hibernate in a snug nest or den until the spring. Why is this such a good idea?

Trees rest in winter, too

Many trees shed their leaves in time for winter, and stop growing. This is the best way for them to survive the cold weather.

It's a good time to see the shapes of different kinds of trees.

Green all winter

Not all trees and plants lose their leaves. Some stay green and glossy. They are called evergreens.

Some evergreens are used as decorations at Christmas. What other winter festivals are there?

Spring is coming

It may still be cold. There may even be snow on the ground. Yet certain signs tell us that spring is coming.

Why do the seasons change? Why does spring always follow winter?

Index